Welcome to Canterbury Cathedral. We very much hope that you have a wonderful visit to this place of pilgrimage – the seat of the Archbishop of Canterbury as Primate of all England, Diocesan Bishop of the diocese of Canterbury, and leader of the Anglican Communion throughout the world. It is both a holy place where worship has been carried on daily for over fourteen hundred years, and part of a World Heritage Site containing many historic treasures. It is also the home of a community made up of many different types of people, all of whom seek to make the Cathedral a place of welcome, beauty and holiness.

There has been a school attached to the Cathedral from the beginning of its life. On the South side of the Precincts you will see the International Study Centre, opened in April 2002 to enable Christian leaders, students, and other visitors to live and study here as part of the Cathedral community. You will find many things of interest, and this short guidebook will assist you as you make your journey around the Cathedral and Precincts.

Robert Willis.

The Very Reverend Robert Willis, Dean of Canterbury

A Walking Guide

Brief History
In AD 597 missionaries from Rome converted the king of Kent to Christianity. Augustine, leader of the mission, was consecrated as Archbishop and his *cathedra* (official seat) was established at Canterbury. The Cathedral has been the seat of the Archbishop of Canterbury ever since.

Introduction

Orientation
You have come through Christ Church Gate and are now in the Precincts of Canterbury Cathedral. The Gate (**1**), restored between 1931 and 1937, is early Tudor, probably built as a memorial to Henry VII's eldest son Arthur, Prince of Wales, who died in 1502 at the age of 16. The shields on the front represent officers of his household and his trusted supporters. The heavy wooden doors were given by Archbishop Juxon in 1663.

Looking at the Cathedral

The rich variety of architectural styles reflects the history of Canterbury Cathedral from the 11th century. From left to right (**2**) you can see the two Western Towers and the Nave, which was rebuilt in the Perpendicular Gothic style from 1377 to 1405; Bell Harry Tower of 1498; and the Romanesque (Norman) Anselm's Tower of 1130. Out of view is the late 12th-century Corona Tower.

Your Tour

You may enter the Cathedral at this point to begin the Interior Tour. Alternatively, turn to the Exterior Tour section later in this book. On occasion, part or all of the Cathedral interior is closed to visitors. The exterior tour will give you another perspective on the building and its history.

Interior Tour

You enter the Cathedral through the South West Porch (**3**). Built in the reign of Henry V (d.1422), it was decorated outside with historical figures by Theodore Pfyffers in 1862. Pause to look at the medieval angels with shields and, above you, the heraldic roof bosses. Go through the doorway. *Please take care to mind the steps* as you pass under the bell tower and into the Nave. Ahead of you is an information desk where audio tours can be rented; to your left, further help and information is also available. Turn right and continue up the centre of the Nave (**4**) until you reach the font on your left.

In the Nave

The marble font (**5**) was given by Bishop Warner of Rochester in 1639. The cover is decorated with the four Evangelists and other Apostles. It was reputedly smashed by the Puritans in 1643, hidden by William Somner, and then repaired after the Restoration of 1660.

Look back down the Nave to see the West Window. It contains 13 portraits of Christ's ancestors, dating from the late 12th century. Most famously, in the bottom row is *Adam Delving*, c.1176 (**6**), one of the oldest pieces of stained glass in Britain. Above are eight English kings from the early 15th century. In the stone tracery at the top are apostles and saints from c.1400.

As you turn back to face the altar, on your right, opposite the font, note the Victorian memorial to George Beaney with its exotic palm trees.

Walk up the Nave towards the altar and dais; stop adjacent to the pulpit. Take a seat for a moment, if you wish.

Compass Rose

The brass Compass Rose (**7**) is the symbol of the world-wide Angican Communion, with Canterbury Cathedral as the Mother Church. The Greek inscription translates as 'The Truth will set you free' (John 8: 32).

Now look up at the strainer arch (**8**). This and others were added in 1495, bracing the columns to take the weight of Bell Harry Tower.

On your left is a
carved and paint-
ed Gothic Revival
pulpit, designed
by George Bodley
in 1898 as a mem-
orial to Dean R.
Payne-Smith. It
features saints
associated with
Canterbury (**9**).
This is the pulpit
used by the
Archbishop at

9   10

Christmas, Easter, and other special occasions.

Pass in front of the pulpit and turn right. Notice on your left two interesting memorials, the first dating from 1612, the second from c.1596 (**10**). This second memorial commemorates Sir James Hales and his son James – the former drowned in the River Stour, the latter was buried at sea.

Go up the first flight of steps in front of you and then down the steps on the left. Facing you are the tombs of two Archbishops – Peckham (1292) and Warham (1532). On your left is John Clerke's Baroque memorial with its famous cherub's head (**11**). Turn right.

11

The Martyrdom

At this actual spot Thomas Becket was murdered, making this the historical heart of the Cathedral. At dusk on 29 December 1170, Henry II's knights burst in through the cloister door behind you. As Becket was preparing for Vespers (Evensong), they violently attacked him with swords, eventually killing him on these stones. From then on this has been a hallowed place of pilgrimage.

The modern version of the *Altar of The Sword's Point* (so-called because a knight's sword tip broke on the stone floor with the ferocity of the blow) is located where a

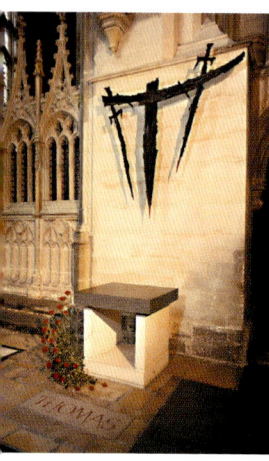

medieval altar stood (**12**). For centuries this has been one of the destinations in the Cathedral to which pilgrims come, originally through the tunnel on your right. Significantly Pope John Paul II and Archbishop Robert Runcie prayed here together on 29 May 1982, during the first ever visit to England by a Pope (**13**). Prayers are still said here by the Archbishop on St Thomas's Day (29 December), after Evensong.

Please read the following paragraph before continuing. You now go downstairs into the Western Crypt where the light levels are very low. The Crypt is a still place; please respect this. The light improves in the Eastern Crypt where the tour resumes.

As you walk ahead you are surrounded by Romanesque architecture. In the North Transept, to the left are the altars of St Nicholas and St Mary Magdalene, a statue of St Thomas, and then the Chapel of the Holy Innocents with its carved pillars. On the right is one of several much larger pillars, added in the 12th century to support the Quire above. Go up a step into the Eastern Crypt, turn right at the conjoined double pillar, go up another step and into the middle.

The Eastern Crypt

The original site of Becket's tomb, from 1170 to 1220, was between the Purbeck marble pillars (**14**). Many miracles of healing are thought to have been performed here. The two latticed windows in the centre, above, allowed monks in the watching chamber to guard the tomb below. Turn round and walk towards the Jesus Chapel. Step down.

The Jesus Chapel

The Eastern Crypt ends in this decorative chapel, one of the most unusual in the Cathedral. In its central window, the rich early glass includes depictions of the Crucifixion and the Madonna and Child. The crowned letters 'M' and 'I' on the restored painted ceiling are the initials of Mary and Jesus in Latin (**15**) – the walls and vault above you show the pattern prior to restoration. Embroidered in 1895, the intricate altar cloth depicts saints associated with Canterbury, including SS Augustine and Alphege, both former archbishops, and has a heading band of angels and lilies of the valley. The floor is made from medieval encaustic tiles, manufactured using different coloured clays on Tyler Hill in Canterbury.

Leaving the Jesus Chapel, turn left and continue into the Romanesque Western Crypt. Go down the step, turn left, then left again, and enter St Gabriel's Chapel.

St Gabriel's Chapel

Here in this chapel are fine examples of 12th-century wall paintings and 11th-century carvings. The paintings above the altar, which were hidden for many years, show Christ in Majesty with Angels. On the left wall you can see scenes depicting the life of St John the Baptist. These contrast with a modern Icon of the Annunciation. Behind you is the Cathedral's best preserved example of a

Romanesque column capital, showing animals and mythical creatures (**16**). Part of the painted ceiling above shows the Crown of Thorns and Tongues of Fire.

Leaving St Gabriel's Chapel turn left, past Archbishop Morton's cenotaph on your right. Turn right when you are beside the doorway to the Huguenot Chapel. Although not generally open to the public, worship in French takes place here every Sunday at 3.00pm.

Chapel of Our Lady Undercroft

You are welcome to sit here and light a candle. Screens of carved and painted stone dating from the 14th century span the Romanesque arches in front of you. Again there is a contrast between old and new – look at the modern bronze statue of *Our Lady of Canterbury* (1982) against the painted ceiling (**17**). However, if you turn round you can see that you are still in the 11th-century crypt that medieval pilgrims would have known, as this chapel was on the route to Becket's shrine.

Walk between these famous columns towards the glass doors of the Silver Treasury. By all means go in if it is open, or turn left and then right to go up the steps to leave the Crypt.

At the top of the steps look up, above the small shop, at the 1902 Christopher Whall window depicting *The Nativity* (**18**), *The Agony in the Garden* and *The Resurrection*. Now turn right and go up the steps towards the Pulpitum Screen.

On the steps beneath Bell Harry Tower

Looking back into the South West Transept, you see the Great Window above the South Door. It features more Old Testament figures in 12th-century glass, including a famous image of Methuselah (**19**) in the bottom row.

Move to the middle of the wide steps and look up. Above you is the lantern vaulting of the crossing tower, Bell Harry, so-called because of the bell at the top (**20**). This spectacular example of fan vaulting, by John Wastell, was finished in 1503 and features the coats of arms of the main benefactors, including Cardinal Morton and Prior Goldstone. The centre is a trap door, above which is the large treadmill used in the construction of the Tower.

Look right at the great Royal Window of the Martyrdom Transept (**21**), showing King Edward IV, his wife, and family, including his daughter Elizabeth, who married Henry VII, and the two tragic 'Princes in the Tower'. Much of the window was deliberately wrecked by Puritan fanatics in 1643. Now turn and go up the steps, looking at the Pulpitum

Screen. 15th-century sculptures show six kings in the niches. From left to right they are: Henry V, Richard II, Ethelbert (**22**), Edward the Confessor, Henry IV, and Henry VI. The Plantagenet kings are thought to be portrait likenesses, possibly carved by John Massingham.

Through the 13th-century iron gates in the centre you enter the Quire. The full length of the earliest Gothic Quire and Trinity Chapel is before you. The High Altar stands on a flight of steps, above which more steps lead to St Augustine's Chair (**23**), probably 13th century, in which archbishops are enthroned as Primate of all England. Walk towards the brass lectern of 1663 (**24**) and look at the differing architectural styles. The external wall is Romanesque, while the arches of the Quire are early Gothic (it was rebuilt after a fire in 1174).

At the Lectern

Directly above the lectern is a roof boss with the Lamb and Flag, a symbol of the Resurrection. William of Sens fell here when scaffolding collapsed in 1178. He was badly injured and died in France. William the Englishman completed his work. Turn left, up two steps, and walk towards the gate. On the right is the tomb of Archbishop Chichele

(d.1443), one of the finest tombs in the Cathedral (**25**).

Go through the gate and turn left, past the large medieval wall painting of c.1480 on the right, telling the legend of St Eustace.

The Bible Windows

Dating from c.1180 these windows are part of a lost series, *The Bible of the Poor* – so-called because the illiterate majority could learn biblical stories from them. The right-hand window has roundels including New Testament Miracles and, on the left, *Noah and the Dove* (**26**). Three of the panels from the left-hand window were copied for the Christmas stamps in 1971, including *The Three Magi* (**27**).

Retrace your steps past the gate, keeping Chichele's tomb on your right. Beyond the North East transept, on your left, is the wrought-iron gate to St Andrew's Chapel. There is no public access, but you can see the painted ceiling of this Romanesque chapel (**28**). A door with three locks, from the 17th century, leads to the *vestiarium* (the current vestry). Proceed *carefully* to the top of the age-worn North steps.

At the top of the North steps

You are now in the North Aisle of the Trinity Chapel. On your left, in the first window of the chapel, is the most famous image of St Thomas (modern, but made from old glass), fully robed as Archbishop and giving a blessing (**29**). Higher up is Becket with his Primatial cross (**30**) and Henry II. All around are the vivid 13th-century Miracle Windows. Some panels show the original tomb in the Crypt (**31**), and others the shrine of 1220, which used to be located on your right. The original site is now marked by a burning candle. It was destroyed on the orders of Henry VIII in 1538 (Becket's cult was one that questioned the King's supremacy in Church matters).

The pavement (floor) of this chapel was prepared for the repositioning of the shrine in 1220 (**32**), and includes an Italian-style geometric, marble mosaic and a series of French roundels, showing seasons and the zodiac. You now get a full sense of the size of St Augustine's Chair, which sits in front of the pavement.

Continue along this aisle past, on your left, the famous Miracle Windows and, on the right, the tomb of King Henry IV and Queen Joan of Navarre (**33**), towards the east end of the Cathedral. Stop in front of the altar of the Corona Chapel.

The Corona Chapel

This chapel was added to house the *corona* (top of the head) of St Thomas, which was struck off when he was martyred. In 1978 the chapel was rededicated to the Saints and Martyrs of our Own Time.

Behind the altar is the 13th-century Redemption Window with, from bottom to top: the Crucifixion, Entombment, Resurrection, Ascension (the diamond panel shows just the feet of Jesus ascending into Heaven); and finally Pentecost. These New Testament events are contrasted with Old Testament stories on all sides, such as the *Grapes of Eshcol* below the Crucifixion. Spies sent into Canaan by Moses, to see if the land was fertile, returned with a huge bunch of grapes (**34**).

To the left is a Tree of Jesse window, and to the right is Victorian glass imitating unrestored medieval glass. If you wish, you can light a candle here. If you turn round, you get a superb view of the entire length of the Cathedral to the West Window (515 feet / 157 metres).

Continuing to your left, you pass a popular image of medieval pilgrims on the road to Canterbury (**35**), in the incomplete third window. Below that is the tomb of Archbishop Hubert Walter, the oldest tomb in the Cathedral. It dates from 1205 and has Romanesque carved heads.

The Black Prince's tomb

Further along on your right is one of the Cathedral's finest medieval tombs, that of Edward, Prince of Wales, known as the Black Prince (d.1376). The gilded effigy shows him in full armour and gauntlets (**36**), including the spurs he won at the battle of Crécy, his dog and helmet. At the top hang copies of his funeral 'achievements'. The shields on the tomb include, for the first time, the three ostrich feathers

of peace, which are still referred to as 'Prince of Wales feathers'. His detailed funeral instructions were followed closely, except that of burial in the Crypt – it was deemed more appropriate to locate the tomb here, close to St Thomas. *Carefully go down the worn Pilgrims' Steps* and enter St Anselm's Chapel on the left.

St Anselm's Chapel

St Anselm died in 1109, and his relics were re-buried in this Romanesque chapel in *c*.1130. The striking modern altar is a gift from Aosta's people using local marble. He is depicted in a 1959 Harry Stammers window (**37**) and in a modern icon (**38**), a gift from the monastery at Bec where Anselm was Prior before becoming Archbishop of Canterbury. Above and to the left of the altar is a wall painting of St Paul at Malta with the viper.

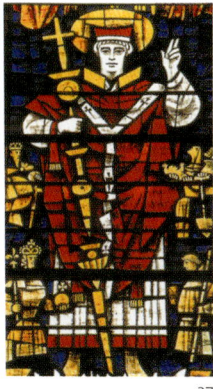

Leaving the Chapel, turn left. Notice the plain window showing how the medieval iron framework holds stained glass in place with triangular iron pegs. Past this is a glass case housing the original 'achievements' of the Black Prince.

South East Transept

There is an interesting collection of visual art here. The four bright windows date from the 1950s. By Ervin Bossanyi, a Hungarian refugee, they explore themes of Peace and Salvation. To their right is a postwar geometric *grisaille* (grey) window, in the style of 13th-century glass (**39**) and acting as a foil to the vivid Bossanyi windows.

Turning back to the two chapels on the left you will find, in the chapel dedicated to St John the Evangelist, a Renaissance oil painting of *The Adoration* by Schidone. The 19th-century glass is part of the Tree of Jesse series.

There is another modern icon in St Gregory's Chapel.

Retrace your steps and continue towards the South West Transept. On the left, below the first memorial (to Dean Neville), is an arcade of three arches (**40**). The left and centre arches are Romanesque, but the right-hand one has been re-carved to early Gothic, to show the new style to the monks. Perhaps this is the first Gothic arch in England.

Further on, in the last window before the steps down, is a panel showing Mary on a donkey in *The Flight to Egypt*. Go down the stairs and turn left.

South West Transept

Facing the Warriors' Chapel of St Michael, you will see to the left the ship's bell of HMS Canterbury. It rings out at 11.00am on weekdays, signalling prayers commemorating the dead of both World Wars and other recent conflicts. In the chapel itself hang many of the old colours of the Buffs (Royal East Kent) Regiment, now The Princess of Wales' Royal Regiment. The altar and East Window are memorials to the men of this Regiment. A page of the *Book of Remembrance* is turned during the daily prayers.

In the centre is the tomb of Lady Margaret Holland (**41**) with her two husbands – John Beaufort, Earl of Somerset (left in the aerial view), and Prince Thomas Plantagenet, Duke of Clarence (right). The chapel was rebuilt by Lady Margaret just before she died in 1439.

You will exit the Cathedral by the South Door, on the path leading towards the International Study Centre and main shop. You now have the choice of taking the exterior tour or leaving the Cathedral Precincts.

The Queen's Golden Jubilee visit, Maundy Thursday, 2002

Exterior Tour

Walk to the West Front of the Cathedral. You will pass the South West Porch with its 1862 niche figures by Theodore Pfyffers. The South West Porch itself is early 15th century.

The West Front

The West Door is used by the Archbishop of Canterbury at Christmas and on other ceremonial occasions. He comes from the Old Palace (the grey flint building on your left), which is his residence when in Canterbury. The majority of the palace is *c.*1900, but recently discovered Romanesque foundations are of Lanfranc's Palace. When in residence, the Archbishop's standard flies from the flagstaff on the tower.

Looking up at the towers of the West Front you see a matching pair – however, they are actually four centuries apart. Arundel Tower, on the left, was built in 1832 to replace Romanesque work by Lanfranc of 1070. This Tower houses the five chiming bells for the clock, as well as Great Dunstan, the heaviest bell at 3185 kilos. The Oxford Tower is the work of Mapilton, from 1434, housing the 14 ringing bells. Between the towers is the tracery of the West Window.

The Great Cloister

Walking round the base of the Arundel Tower, with its recently carved gargoyles, go down the ramp and steps to the Great Cloister. Here, on the vaulting, are ornate roof bosses, some representing a rich array of late medieval English heraldry (**42**). Below are the tombstones of people associated with the Cathedral's history. On your right are

stone benches with medieval games and graffiti carved into them. On your left, through the bays, are the tombs of some of the archbishops, the lawn, and the far side of the rectangular Cloister. Walk towards the doorway in front of you, and stop once there. Notice how the 15th-century vault ribbing cuts through the 13th-century stonework. This doorway was elaborately decorated because it leads to the site of Becket's Martyrdom. Turn left, walk on for a short distance, and turn right through the glass doors into the Chapter House.

42

The Chapter House

This building, the walls of which date from the late 11th century, was named after the first item of business at the daily monastic meeting – the Prior, from his throne, would read out a chapter of the rules of St Benedict. The current governing body of the Cathedral also takes its name from this.

The superb wagon-vaulted roof of c.1400 (**43**) is made from Irish oak, and its decoration is typical of late English Gothic style. The two main windows are late Victorian, and the subject matter of one is mirrored in the other (for instance, bottom right in both windows is Queen Victoria). Other depictions include the four national saints

and scenes from British history. This is the largest Chapter House in England. More recently it was the scene of the signing of the Channel Tunnel treaty, in 1986, by British Prime Minister Margaret Thatcher and French President François Mitterand.

Turn right as you exit. After a few steps turn right again into the passage, leaving the Great Cloister, and pass the door of the Library and Archives on your left. You walk between thick, decorated, Romanesque pillars towards the Water Tower. Step left through the arches, onto the paved area surrounding the Water Tower.

The Water Tower and environs

Built in the 12th century by Prior Wibert, this was the centre of the monastic water supply (**44**). The upper part of the tower was a cistern, supported by finely carved Romanesque columns (which were buttressed at a later date). It did not originally have windows.

To the right of the Tower, look up on the wall of the Cathedral to a small blocked-off doorway. This was used by the monks at night for entrance to services. Keep turning and look at the exterior of the Cathedral Library, rebuilt after bombing in 1942. To the right, opposite the Cathedral, you can see through to Green Court.

Heading back towards the Cathedral, you will find the disabled access points for the Crypt (down a slope) and the lift for the Quire, past the Dean's Steps on your right. On the wall at the corner of this smaller cloister is a good map of the old Priory. Turn the corner, through the iron gate, and walk a few steps towards the open doorway on your right. Look left at the patterned arches (**45**) of the old cloister. Look straight ahead through to the Prior's Gatehouse before going through the doorway. On your right are great Romanesque arches of the ruined monks'

infirmary (**46**), which leads on to the infirmary Chapel. On the left is a fine 17th-century house, with hermaphroditic carvings supporting the first-floor bay window. Turn right opposite it, and follow the path towards the Corona Tower (below).

The Corona Tower

This is unfinished, hence the huge buttresses that point up to the sky (**47**). There were several plans for this, including a tall spire, which never materialised. It was built by 1184 as the final work of William the Englishman, completing the project begun by William of Sens (d.1180). Here you can see the oldest Romanesque exterior, that of the two Eastern transepts. Behind you is a gate through to the Kent County Memorial Gardens and on to the Queningate, so-called because Queen Bertha used it to go to St Martin's Church.

Follow the path round the outside of the Cathedral. The small chapel before the large South East Transept is St Anselm's Chapel. The curved apse of its eastern end (**48; left**) marks the extent of the Romanesque cathedral that St Thomas would have known. The Gothic window above now houses a 1959 window by Harry Stammers (**48; right**). Walk down a small path towards a door in the South East Transept, which leads to the Huguenot Chapel.

Huguenot Chapel

This was originally the Black Prince's Chantry, where he expected to be buried, but his tomb is in a place of honour in the Trinity Chapel. Queen Elizabeth I gave this chapel to the refugee French Protestant Huguenots, who first fled to Britain over 400 years ago, and again in the late 17th century when persecuted by Louis XIV. Services are still held here in French every Sunday afternoon. Walk towards the door and look up at the carved arcades of Romanesque arches. These alternate between a decorated column shaft or column capital and are superb examples of architecture *c.*1100 (far right of **48**).

The South Precincts

Walking back to the main path, this is roughly the point where the Precincts were divided by a gate between monastic privacy to the east and public access to the west. To the right of the South West Transept is the modified chapel to St Michael. The small protruding piece of stonework is part of Archbishop Stephen Langton's tomb, which was exposed by Lady Margaret Holland rebuilding the chapel in 1439.

If you stand at the end of the path out of the South West Transept and look up, you will see a small tower on the left. This is the Candle Tower, with wonderful gargoyles (**49**). It was completely re-carved and replaced in 2000.

Leaving the Precincts

On your left is the International Study Centre. This award-winning building, by Sir William Whitfield, was completed in 2000 and represents the most significant building in the Precincts for 400 years. It houses a 250-seat auditorium, conference facility and lodge (**50**) and is a resource for the Cathedral, the City of Canterbury, and the worldwide Anglican Communion.

Go up the slope beside the International Study Centre. On the right is a vista of old buildings with peg-tiled roofs, including Cathedral House, formerly a Canon's house. Look back now for a superb view of the Cathedral and Bell Harry Tower (**51**).

50 51

SERVICE TIMES

Sundays

Holy Communion	8.00am
Matins said (or sung by the King's School)	9.30am
Sung Eucharist (with sermon)	11.00am
Choral Evensong	3.15pm
Evening service (with sermon)	6.30pm

Weekdays

Matins	7.30am
Holy Communion	8.00am
Holy Communion (Major Saints' Days)	11.15am
Holy Communion (Wednesday)	11.15am
Choral Evensong	5.30pm
Holy Communion (Thursday)	6.15pm

Saturdays

Holy Communion	8.00am
Matins	9.30am
Choral Evensong	3.15pm

Information correct at time of going to press: June 2015

OPENING TIMES FOR GENERAL VISITING
9.00am – 5.30pm (summer); 9.00am – 4.30pm (winter);
12.30pm – 2.30pm (Sundays)
Access is limited at the times of the services
N.B. The Cathedral or parts of it may have to close from time to time for special circumstances without prior notice

GUIDED TOURS
Only accredited Cathedral Guides are permitted to operate in the Cathedral
One hour General Guided Tours take place throughout the day. Special Tours of an extended duration may be arranged in advance throughout the year. Advance bookings by groups and foreign language tours can be arranged.
Audio tours in seven languages are available, starting from the west end of the Nave. Audio-visual presentations by prior arrangement.
For further details, contact the VISITS OFFICE,
11 The Precincts, Canterbury, Kent CT1 2EH
Tel: 01227 762 862; Fax: 01227 865 222
Email: visits@canterbury-cathedral.org
Website: **www.canterbury-cathedral.org**

CANTERBURY CATHEDRAL SHOP
25 Burgate, Canterbury, Kent CT1 2HA
9.30am – 5.30pm Monday to Saturday
10.30am – 4.30pm on Sunday
Tel: 01227 865 300; Fax: 01227 865 333
Email: **enquiries@cathedral-enterprises.co.uk**
Website: **www.cathedral-enterprises.co.uk**

© Scala Arts & Heritage Publishers Ltd, 2015
Text by Pam Wintle & Chris Needham © Cathedral Enterprises Ltd., with thanks to Margaret Sparks for historical accuracy.

Published by Scala Arts & Heritage Publishers Ltd, 10 Lion Yard, Tremadoc Road, London SW4 7NQ. Printed & bound in China. All rights reserved. No part of this book may be reproduced, stored in a retrieval system or transmitted in any form or by any means electronic, mechanical, photocopying or otherwise, without the written permission of Scala Arts & Heritage Publishers Ltd.

ISBN-13: 978-0-906211-53-3 / ISBN-10: 0-906211-53-0

PICTURE CREDITS (image numbers refer to stops on the tour)
© **Robert Greshoff/CEL**: Front cover, inside front cover, inside back cover.
© **CEL**: Welcome page, 1, 4, 5, 7, 8, 9, 11, 12, 13, 14, 15, 16, 17, 18, 23, 24, 25, 36, 38, 39, 41, HM the Queen 2002, 42, 45, 46, 47. © **Dominique Levet**: 3, 28.
© **Angelo Hornak**: 6, 10, 19, 20, 21, 22, 27, 29, 30, 32, 33, 34, 35, 40, 43, 44, 48, 49, 50, 51. © **Sonia Halliday**: 26, 31. © **Dean and Chapter of Canterbury, Stained Glass Department**: 37. © **Chris Schwartz**: 2.
Back cover and flap collage images by **CEL**, **David Manners**, **Mary Tucker**, **Brian Winter** and **Lisa Emanuel**. Plan by **ML Design**. Thanks to all.